3382 5638

W9-CFV-447

Florida

A Buddy Book
by
Julie Murray

ABDO
Publishing Company

VISIT US AT
www.abdopub.com

Published by ABDO Publishing Company, 4940 Viking Drive, Edina, Minnesota 55435.

Printed in the United States.

Edited by: Sarah Tieck
Contributing Editor: Michael P. Goecke
Graphic Design: Deb Coldiron, Maria Hosley
Image Research: Sarah Tieck
Photographs: Clipart.com, Corbis, Getty Images, Library of Congress, Michael P. Goecke, One Mile Up, Photos.com, SuperStock

Library of Congress Cataloging-in-Publication Data

Murray, Julie, 1969-
   Florida / Julie Murray.
      p. cm. — (The United States)
   Includes bibliographical references and index.
   ISBN 1-59197-668-5
      1. Florida—Juvenile literature. I. Title.

F311.3.M87 2005
975.9—dc22

2004050229

Table Of Contents

A Snapshot Of Florida

Florida has warm weather and sunny days all through the year. This is why Florida is known as the "Sunshine State."

There are 50 states in the United States. Every state is different. Every state has an official state nickname.

Florida became a United States territory in 1822. Florida worked to become a state for many years. Finally, it became the 27th state on March 3, 1845.

Many people travel to Florida because it has so many sunny days.

Florida covers 58,681 square miles (146,803 sq km) of land. Florida is the 22nd-largest state in the United States. It is home to 15,982,378 people.

Florida is a long, flat state. Most of Florida is a peninsula. The northwestern part of the state is called the Panhandle. This name comes from the shape of the land. The Panhandle is along the Gulf of Mexico. It is shaped like the handle on a frying pan.

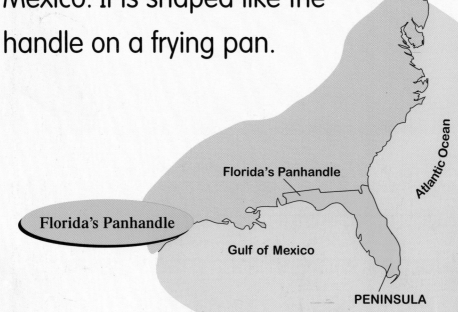

Florida's Panhandle

Florida's Panhandle

Gulf of Mexico

Atlantic Ocean

PENINSULA

The pink flamingo is a type of bird that lives in Florida.

Where Is Florida?

There are four parts of the United States. Each part is called a region. Each region is in a different area of the country. The United States Census Bureau says the four regions are the Northeast, the South, the Midwest, and the West. Florida is in the South region of the United States.

Four Regions of the United States of America

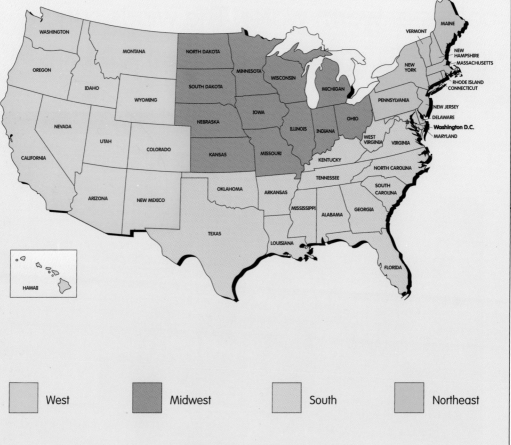

West   Midwest   South   Northeast

Florida has hot, humid weather. People living in Florida have to be prepared for hurricanes. A hurricane is a powerful storm. It can form by swirling over large bodies of warm water. The winds can be as high as 200 miles (322 km) per hour.

In Florida, hurricanes can happen between June and November.

Florida is bordered by two states. Georgia lies to the north. Alabama is to the north and northwest. The Atlantic Ocean borders the state on the east. The Gulf of Mexico is west.

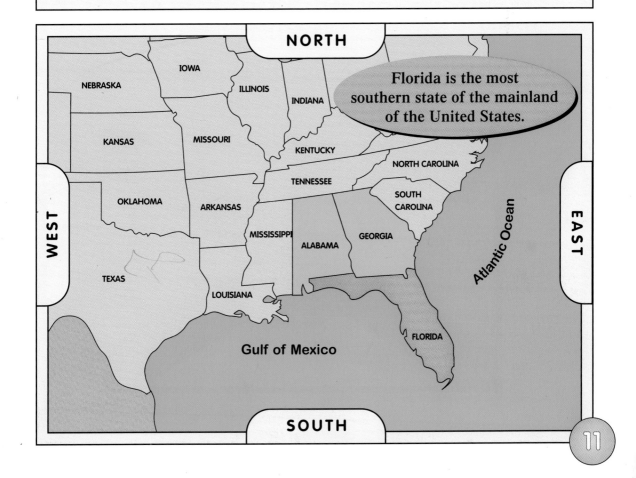

NORTH

IOWA

NEBRASKA

ILLINOIS

INDIANA

Florida is the most southern state of the mainland of the United States.

KANSAS

MISSOURI

KENTUCKY

NORTH CAROLINA

TENNESSEE

SOUTH CAROLINA

WEST

OKLAHOMA

ARKANSAS

MISSISSIPPI

GEORGIA

Atlantic Ocean

EAST

ALABAMA

TEXAS

LOUISIANA

FLORIDA

Gulf of Mexico

SOUTH

Florida

State abbreviation: FL

State nickname: The Sunshine State

State capital: Tallahassee

State motto: In God we trust

Statehood: March 3, 1845, 27th state

Population: 15,982,378, ranks 4th

State flag:
Adopted in 1899

Land area: 58,681 square miles (146,803 sq km), ranks 22nd

State tree: Sabal palm

State song: "Old Folks At Home" ("Swanee River")

State government: Three branches: legislative, executive, and judicial

Average July temperature: 81°F (27°C)

Average January temperature: 59°F (15°C)

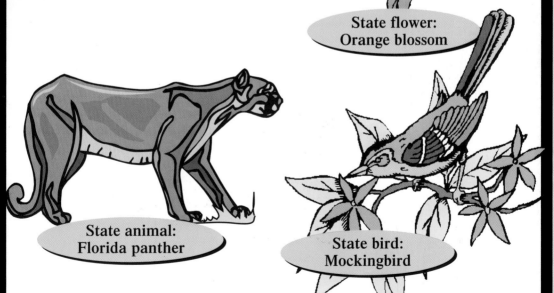

State flower: Orange blossom

State animal: Florida panther

State bird: Mockingbird

Cities And The Capital

Tallahassee is in the northern part of Florida. It has been the capital of Florida since 1824. The name Tallahassee is from a Native American word. It means "old town."

Jacksonville is Florida's largest city. It is located in northern Florida. Jacksonville is named after former president Andrew Jackson. The city is home to many businesses. Also, many sports are played in Jacksonville.

Miami is known for its beaches and its nightlife. It is a popular tourist spot.

Miami is the second-largest city in Florida. Miami is home to the Orange Bowl. It is played on or near New Year's Day each year.

Famous Citizens

Sidney Poitier (1927–)

There are many famous people from Florida. Sidney Poitier is one. He was born in Miami in 1927. He was one of the first famous African-American actors to play leading roles. He was known for movies such as *Guess Who's Coming to Dinner.* He won an Academy Award in 1964 for *Lilies of the Field.*

Sidney Poitier

Famous Citizens

Tennessee Williams (1911–1983)

Tennessee Williams was a famous playwright. He was not born in Florida, but he lived in Florida for more than 30 years. Tennessee Williams was born in Mississippi in 1911. He moved to Key West in 1949. While living in Florida, he won a Pulitzer Prize. Tennessee Williams is known for *The Glass Menagerie*, *A Streetcar Named Desire*, and *Cat on a Hot Tin Roof*.

Tennessee Williams

Everglades National Park

Everglades National Park covers 1,508,538 acres (610,484 ha) of wetland. This area is in southern Florida. It is the largest swamp in the United States. Mangrove trees and tall razor-like grass grows throughout the Everglades. Alligators, crocodiles, panthers, herons, and snakes live there.

Alligators live in the Everglades.

A great blue heron

Everglades National Park was created in 1947. Today, it is the largest national park east of the Rocky Mountains. More than one million people visit every year. Also, visitors can take airboat rides through the Everglades. There are boardwalks to safely view the area.

Tourist Attractions

Florida is one of the most visited states in the country. Tourists come from all over the world to visit the Sunshine State. There are many tourist attractions in Florida.

Orlando is the home to Walt Disney World. Walt Disney World is one of the world's most visited theme parks. Walt Disney World includes more than one theme park. There is EPCOT, the Magic Kingdom, Disney-MGM Studios, and Disney's Animal Kingdom Park.

John F. Kennedy Space Center is where the United States launches space shuttles. It is located on Merritt Island. People can visit Kennedy Space Center. There they learn about space exploration, spacecrafts, and the astronauts.

Other destinations include beaches, golf courses, zoos, theme parks, and spring-training baseball to name a few.

Sometimes visitors can watch a space shuttle taking off at Kennedy Space Center.

Animals Of Florida

Many animals live in Florida. Sea turtles, dolphins, pelicans, and flamingos are just a few.

Alligators and crocodiles are both found in Florida. It is the only place in the United States that these two reptiles are found together. They live at the state's southern tip in marshes. Alligators can often be seen sunning themselves on rocks or on the shore. Crocodiles are not often seen. They are on the endangered animal list.

Alligator

An alligator's long mouth is
wider than a crocodile's.

Crocodile

Other endangered animals live in Florida, too. People don't see these animals very often. They are in danger of dying out.

The Florida panther is an endangered animal. It is large and brown or tawny. It is part of the mountain lion family.

The Florida panther is Florida's state mammal.

Manatees are sometimes called sea cows.

Manatees are also endangered animals. They are big marine mammals. They have two small flippers in the front. A manatee can weigh as much as 3,500 pounds (1,588 kg). They can eat more than 100 pounds (45 kg) of plants in one day.

Florida

Juan Ponce de León

1513: Juan Ponce de León arrives in Florida. He was a Spanish explorer. He named it La Florida.

1822: Florida becomes a United States territory.

1845: Florida becomes the 27th state on March 3.

1969: Florida's legislature ratifies the 19th Amendment. This is the amendment that guaranteed all women the right to vote.

1971: Walt Disney World's Magic Kingdom opens.

Walt Disney World

George W. Bush (left) ran for president against Al Gore (right).

1992: Hurricane Andrew hits in August.

2000: Republican candidate George W. Bush and Democratic candidate Al Gore run for president. There are voting problems in Florida. These cause delays. People do not know who is elected president for five weeks after the election.

2004: Four hurricanes hit Florida during a six-week period. These include Hurricane Charley, Hurricane Frances, Hurricane Ivan, and Hurricane Jeanne.

Cities in Florida

Pensacola

Tallahassee ★

● Jacksonville

Orlando ●

● Cape Canaveral

Sarasota ●

● Fort Myers

● Miami

Key West

Important Words

capital a city where government leaders meet.

endangered in danger of dying out.

humid air that is moist or damp.

hurricane a storm that forms over warm seawater with winds more than 74 miles (119 km) per hour.

mammal most living things that belong to this special group have hair, give birth to live babies, and make milk to feed their babies.

nickname a name that describes something special about a person or a place.

peninsula a long piece of land that juts into the sea. A peninsula is joined to a bigger landmass.

swamp a wet, soggy piece of land.

Web Sites

To learn more about Florida, visit ABDO Publishing Company on the World Wide Web. Web site links about Florida are featured on our Book Links page. These links are routinely monitored and updated to provide the most current information available.

www.abdopub.com

Index